A PROJECTIVE T[OOL]

BUBBLE STORIES

FOR WORKING WITH KIDS

By Scott Stella M.S. MFTI

DESIGN TEAM
Scott Stella • Ken Sampson

© 2011 by YouthLight, Inc.

YouthLight, Inc.
P.O. Box 115
Chapin, SC 29036
800-209-9774
www.youthlightbooks.com

All rights reserved. No part of this book may be reproduced or transmitted in any form or by any means, electronic or mechanical, including photocopying and recording, or by any information storage or retrieval system without written permission of the publisher.

ISBN: 978-1-59850-100-1

Library of Congress Number
2011920213

Special Design Assistance from Amy Rule

10 9 8 7 6 5 4 3 2 1
Printed in the United States

ACKNOWLEDGEMENTS

For My Daughter Lily...

Never Lose Touch With Your Inner Child.
Remember That Magical Time of Innocence and
Enchantment Before We All Turn Into Grown Ups.

Great Thanks to Ken Sampson for All his Work and
for Making this Book Possible.

Ken Sampson grew up in a small mountain town.
He has since practiced various forms of art in various parts of the world.

BUBBLE STORIES... WHAT IS THAT?

Children from the ages of 6-16 often lack the verbal skills or emotional vocabulary to communicate in a therapeutic setting. In addition, children may be uncomfortable with direct verbal disclosure of significant events and experiences.

BUBBLE STORIES is a unique, never used before projective technique for working with children, and gaining insight into the child's inner world. **BUBBLE STORIES** consist of cartoon-like drawings with the word and thought bubbles left blank. The object of the exercise is for the child to fill in the bubbles with whatever comes to mind. Younger children can respond verbally, use stickers, color or draw on the pictures.

BUBBLE STORIES is NOT a diagnostic method of personality assessment, instead, the purpose of the exercise is to give therapists another tool to facilitate discussion and build rapport with children. The pictures are purposely designed in black and white and without a lot of background, environmental cues that might distract the child from dealing with the picture content at hand.

The workbook is separated into four main sections: Family, School, Internal Stuff & External Stuff. The family scenarios may show a family sitting at the kitchen table, or a child being scolded. The school scenes might portray a child not paying attention in class, or a kid being rejected by classmates. The internalized section will contain images of a child crying, or a kid looking glum while others are having fun. The externalized scenarios will depict scenes such as a big kid picking on a smaller kid, or a kid destroying property.

BUBBLE STORIES... WHO IS IT FOR?

BUBBLE STORIES are to be used with boys and girls between the ages of 6-16. Younger children who are unable to write responses in the comic bubbles are encouraged to tell the therapist what the child or adult in the picture is saying or thinking. Older children can write the responses directly in the bubbles.

This workbook is designed to help any child that is brought into counseling for treatment. Children exhibiting a variety of presenting problems such as depression, anxiety, grief, self-esteem, attachment difficulties, as well as, family and school issues will benefit from **BUBBLE STORIES**.

BUBBLE STORIES... WHO CAN DO THE EXERCISES WITH CHILDREN?

It is recommended that individuals who are interested in doing the **BUBBLE STORIES** exercises with children have adequate training in psychotherapy, multicultural counseling and child development. A therapist having a Degree in counseling, psychology, family therapy, social work or some other area of the helping profession with the emphasis on the clinical or counseling aspects of the therapeutic relationship is a general prerequisite.

The therapist should be cautious when using **BUBBLE STORIES** interactive approach since the exercise is interactive and subjective in nature, the therapist must be aware of the child's background and think carefully about making interpretations in order to provide the child with an unconditional and nonjudgmental environment.

Other important qualifications for any therapist working with children would include: having an open mind, a great imagination and never losing touch with their own inner child.

BUBBLE STORIES... HOW TO DO THE EXERCISES?

Although **BUBBLE STORIES** can be done just about anywhere and in any way that is therapeutic, but I will make a few recommendations. In terms of the physical setting, obtain or arrange furniture that enables both the therapist and the child to sit on an equal level. This may mean both sitting on the floor, on cushions, or on small chairs if feasible. It is also advisable to avoid sitting behind a desk as this may remind children of authority figures in their life and discourage their trust. Other objects in the room such as books and photos should be analyzed for their impression on the child.

In order to keep the child engaged emotionally, this exercise should be used in concert with other traditional child therapy approaches such as play and art therapy. It would be unadvisable to have the child fill in too many scenes in a short period of time as this would tax the child, and prevent the therapist from exploring meaningful moments with the child.

The therapist can also get a lot of information from other factors apart from the words the child writes in the Bubbles such as level of comfort or resistance, as well as, the non verbal cues while doing the exercise. The trained clinician has the responsibility to delicately process what is revealed, make supportive comments, and offer encouragement.

As clinicians begin to use **BUBBLE STORIES** in practice, I would recommend checking in with the child periodically to see what their experiences are as they do the exercises. Do they roll their eyes when you bring out the workbook? Do they avoid any emotionally charged pictures? Or do they seem pleased to have another way of expressing themselves?

BUBBLE STORIES... IMPORTANT NOTE:

A single means of evaluating an individual has the potential for distortion and misrepresentation. Any information generated through projective devices requires substantiation from additional sources (i.e. behavioral observations, expressed statements of the client, school reports, and interviews with family). By having additional intervention options, the child can be offered more activities to choose from and this may prevent the boredom that comes from using the same standard therapeutic products. Also, using different therapeutic tools in concert with other diagnostic measures may provide a better understanding of the child and provide a means to advance the counseling relationship.

There has been a good deal of research on the effectiveness of psychotherapy with children, but it is impossible to know what will work, and with whom. Psychotherapy has been called a "Behavioral Science", but I believe working with children is more art than science. The **BUBBLE STORIES** can be a small part of helping children express themselves only if they are used by a therapist who has a genuine acceptance, and an unconditional regard for the child. It is this positive therapeutic alliance that allows the to have a genuine experience of the self.

CONTENTS

FAMILY 1

SCHOOL 19

INTERNAL STUFF 32

EXTERNAL STUFF 43

PAGE 2

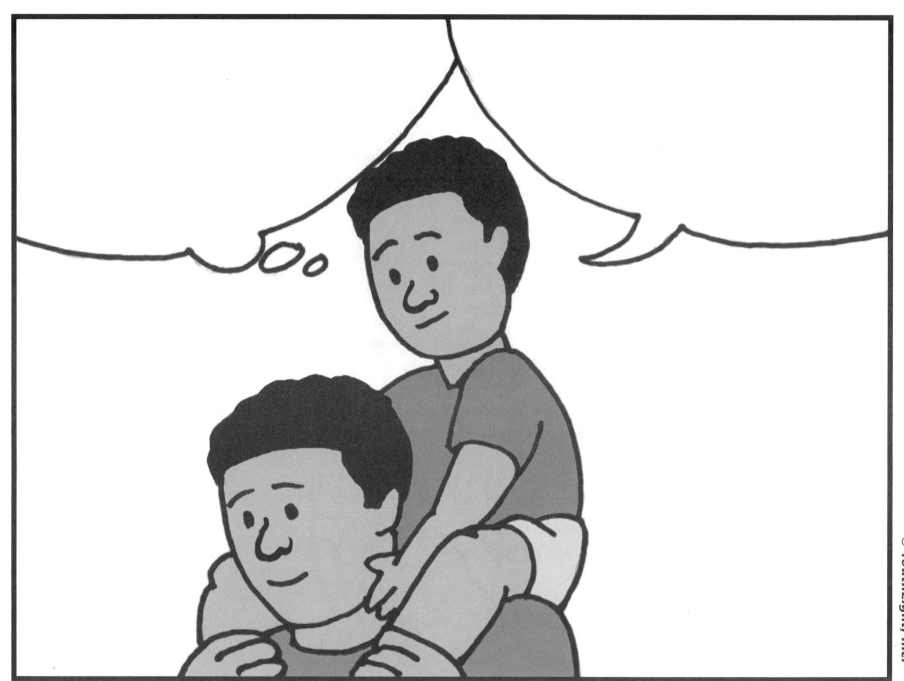

PAGE 12

PAGE 26

PAGE 36